The Salient Art Of Forgiveness

Discovering Inner Peace Through The Power Of Forgiveness

Sensei Paul David

Copyright Page

The Salient Art Of Forgiveness: Discovering Inner Peace Through The Power Of Forgiveness,
by Sensei Paul David

Copyright © 2021

All rights reserved.

978-1-77848-015-7 The Salient Art Of Forgiveness - Ingram Paperback Book
978-1-77848-014-0 The Salient Art Of Forgiveness - Amazon Paperback Book
978-1-77848-013-3 The Salient Art Of Forgiveness - Amazon eBook

This book is not authorized for free distribution copying.

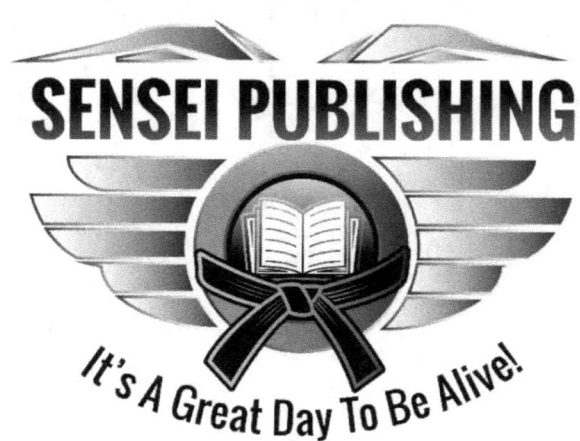

www.senseipublishing.com

@senseipublishing
#senseipublishing

Get/Share Our FREE All-Ages Mental Health Book Now!

FREE Self-Development Book for Every Family

senseiselfdevelopment.senseipublishing.com

Click Below or Search Amazon for Another Book In This Series

senseiselfdevelopment.senseipublishing.com

Join Our Publishing Journey!

If you would like to receive FUTURE FREE BOOKS, and get to know us better, please click www.senseipublishing.com and join our newsletter by entering your email address in the pop-up box.

Follow Our Blog: senseipauldavid.ca

Follow/Like/Subscribe: Facebook, Instagram, YouTube: @senseipublishing

Scan the QR Code with your phone or tablet
to follow us on social media: Like / Subscribe / Follow

Thank You from The Author: Sensei Paul David

Before we dive in, I would like to thank you for picking up this book from among the many other similar books out there. Thank you for choosing to invest in my book. That means everything to me.

Now that you are here, I ask you to stick with me as we take your self-discovery journey together. I promise to make our time together valuable and worthwhile.

In the pages ahead, you will find some areas of information and practices more helpful than others - and that is great! I encourage you to apply what works best for you. You will benefit from the knowledge that you gain and the ensuing exciting transformation of character.Enjoy!

FOREWORD

Forgiveness is the key to living a life devoid of negative emotions. For one reason or the other, this art that is meant to be ubiquitous is so elusive. In *The Salient Art Of Forgiveness*, Paul reminds us about the importance of this art and how its practice can help us to live the meaningful and happy life we all desire.

Like an expert builder, he begins by laying solid foundations by helping us to understand the concept. Like a seasoned guide, he holds us by the hand and leads us into why we need to forgive others and ourselves. Like a loving father, he reminds us about the importance of forgiving ourselves as a precursor to forgiving others.

In this book, like a patient life coach, Paul equips us with the skills to forgive others and ourselves, even before there is an offence, which is very critical. He concludes the book by teaching us how we can avoid offending others and also reduce the chances of others hurting us. *The Salient Art Of Forgiveness* reminds us, once again, why many believe that Paul is one of the best self-help writers out there. This is a must-read for anyone who wants to live a meaningful and happy life.

Contents

FOREWORD vii

Introduction 1

Chapter One: The Art and Practice Of Forgiveness 3

   The Art Of Forgiveness 3
   Forgiveness Can Be Taught And Learned 5
   Every Offence Is A Test 7
   An Offence Is a Blessing In Disguise 9
   The Practice Of Forgiveness 10

Chapter Two: Why You Should Forgive 12

   Maintenance Of Valuable Relationships 13
   Expression Of Empathy 14
   Stability In Relationships 15
   Physical And Mental Heart 17
   Inner Peace 18
   Personal Happiness 19

Chapter Three: Forgiving Yourself 21

   You Are Fallible 21
   There Are Others Like You 23
   Learn The Lessons 24
   Take Responsibility 26
   You Can Still Turn Things Around 27

Chapter Four: Forgiving Others 29

   Forgiveness Is Not A Sign Of Weakness 29
   The People You Love Hurt You More 31
   Find Out Why 32
   Do It For Yourself 34
   Be Willing To Try Again 35

Chapter Five: Law Of Advance Forgiveness....38

- Expect To Be Offended 39
- Think The Unthinkable 40
- Realize The Fallibility Of Your Loved Ones 41
- Plan To Forgive Ahead 42
- Refuse To Give Up On Your Relationships 44
- Always Seek Reconciliation 45

Chapter Six: Avoiding Offences........................ 47

- Clear Expectations 48
- Clear Communication 49
- Listen More 50
- Let What Matters To Others Matter To You 52
- Develop The Heart Of a Servant 53

Chapter Seven: Reducing Chances Of Getting Hurt 55

- Make Reasonable Demands..55
- Be Willing To Compromise 57
- Keep Communicating.. 58
- Train Before Delegating 60
- Test Before Trusting.. 61

Chapter Eight: Just Be Happy! 63

- Forgive! Forgive!! Forgive!!! And Forgive Again 63
- Vengeance Is Not An Option..65
- Stay Away From Vengeful People 67
- Make Friends That Encourage You To Forgive 68
- Keep Unrepentant People At Arm's Length................... 69

Conclusion 71

References 73

Introduction

"To forgive is to set a prisoner free and to discover that the prisoner was you."
Lewis Smedes

This is such a beautiful quote, that is just perfect for the beginning of this journey. When you refuse to forgive, you put yourself in bondage. Unknown to many people, they have the power to let go but they won't. When people hurt us, sometimes we forget that we have also hurt others at certain points in our lives.

Offences are inevitable and we have to always prepare our minds to forgive people. This book is not all about forgiving others. It is way beyond that. It is a complete guide that will teach you how to forgive others and also forgive yourself. It is full of proven techniques that can help you see offences from the right perspective and improve your ability to let go.

When you don't forgive, you bear a burden that will continue to interfere with your happiness. *The Salient Art Of Forgiveness* will teach you how to forgive and also give you tips that will help you to avoid offending others. It will also equip you with hacks that can help you reduce the chances of getting hurt by the people around you.

Chapter One: The Art and Practice Of Forgiveness

"Forgive others not because they deserve forgiveness, but because you deserve peace."
Jonathan Huie

Forgiveness is not only a practice, it is also an art. It is a practice because you will have to do it and it is an art because you have to learn and master it. Forgiveness is not automatic; it is something you do deliberately because you know how to go about it. In this chapter, we will explore forgiveness as an art and a practice.

The Art Of Forgiveness

When it comes to forgiveness, there are two extremes. Some people feel that it is so simple to forgive while some feel that it is extremely difficult or even impossible to forgive. None of the two extremes is accurate enough. Forgiveness is not something simple because it involves your emotions. The fact that you have to choose between either forgiving or refusing to forgive, already tells you that someone has done something that hurt you.

Forgiveness is an art you have to learn. Many of us attend schools and skill acquisition centres so that we can acquire knowledge and skills, but many have never enrolled in the school of forgiveness. Guess what? Admission is free in this school and it is always open to new students. You have to choose to educate yourself regarding the ability to let go of offences because it plays a vital role in your life.

Note that you have to learn to forgive others and also yourself. Both are crucial because it can be devastating if you don't master the two. Failure to forgive yourself can lead to suicidal ideation while refusing to forgive others will ruin your inner peace. So, as you enroll in the college of forgiveness, ensure that you complete the two courses on forgiving yourself and forgiving others. The year 2004 showed that forgiveness has impressive health and social benefits.

Forgiveness Can Be Taught And Learned

The good news is that you can learn to forgive yourself and others. This is the reason I wrote this book. I have discovered in my journey and research that it is possible to improve your ability to forgive. It comes with getting the right information and understanding that will enable you to see things from the right perspective. One of the crucial things you need to understand about forgiveness is that it is not something you do for the benefit of others but yourself to benefit from.

Don't let the overemphasis on Karma mislead you. Good and bad things happen to all. What I mean is that bad things happen to good people and good things happen to bad people. Sometimes, some people you feel don't deserve success. achieve it while some nice people you know go through turbulent times. So, don't get the wrong notion that the people that hurt you would always struggle in life.

If you are sincere and observant enough, you will notice that bad things happen to some of the people that treat you well. I know some nice people that lost their kids. A particularly wonderful couple that were my friends, lost their first child during the process of trying to give birth to him. We should console such people instead of thinking that they are getting the reward for some terrible things they did in the past.

Some years ago, a lady friend was raped by a guy she trusted. She was just a teenager and she felt so disappointed. Unfortunately, it led to pregnancy and she had to choose to abort the child. She hated the guy and wished him only evil. Interestingly, she noticed that the guy was making progress, but she was stagnant in her life. When she told me about the incident, I consoled her. Then I helped her to understand that forgiveness is not something we do for others but for our benefit. She heeded my counsel and forgave the guy, and she began to notice that she was happier and was making progress in her own life too.

Every Offence Is A Test

There is no forgiveness unless there is an offence. In other words, there wouldn't be any need to forgive if someone had not offended you. So, what reveals your ability to forgive others is when they have offended you. Once upon a time, my colleague told me about his boss. He said she was so nice and treated him well. He expected me to commend and praise his boss also but instead, I replied with a question: "Have you ever offended her before?"

He was shocked because he didn't expect the question. He thought for a few seconds and replied, "No." Then I said, "Wait till the day you offend her." I didn't give that response because I doubted the motive or generosity of his boss but because I know that you cannot understand how much someone loves or likes you until you have offended that person. Unknown to many of us, every offence is a test.

When people offend you, it is an opportunity to show them how much you love them. When you struggle to forgive a person, it is a sign that you have never rated them highly or your reasons for caring about them were built on faulty foundations. You should expect people to offend you. Why? They are not perfect. The way you treat people around you when they offend you is the true test of your ability to forgive. Meanwhile, your ability to forgive is the test of your love for others.

An Offence Is a Blessing In Disguise

I try, as much as possible, not to hurt my loved ones but I know that it is bound to happen, sometimes. My experience in life has taught me that an offence is a blessing in disguise. There was a particular day I was joking with a lady friend. I saw a joke that made me laugh and I decided to share it with her. I never knew that she would see it as offensive.

When I told her the joke, she was offended but to my surprise, she began to insult me and told me that she had only been tolerating me before then. I had thought that we were friends but the event made me realize that she never rated me as such at all. From that point on, we stopped talking, not because I was offended but because I realized that I needed to be careful around her.

Meanwhile, it is never a good thing when you have to be careful around your friends. Your friends shouldn't tolerate you; they should accept you. A true friend will overlook your moments of foolishness and choose to forgive you. I realized that she was not my friend and I had to stay away to avoid upsetting her again.

The Practice Of Forgiveness

Forgiveness is firstly an art you need to master but it is also something you need to practice. Whatever you know or understand about forgiveness is irrelevant if you fail to practice it. You need to learn about forgiveness and acquire the necessary hacks that will enable you to practice it effectively.

Yet, you must be more concerned about actually practicing it. Knowledge becomes useful and valuable when it is used to solve problems. You will always find yourself in a situation where you will need to forgive yourself or forgive others. Ensure that you take advantage of those opportunities to display how much you have learned regarding the art of forgiveness.

Chapter Two: Why You Should Forgive

"Never forget the three powerful resources you always have available to you: love, prayer, and forgiveness."
H. Jackson Brown

When you understand the benefits of doing something, it will give you more reasons to master and practice it. We commit to regular exercise because we are convinced that it would improve our physical health and fitness. In the same way, there are several advantages you will enjoy when you choose to forgive. Based on research and personal experience, below are some of the benefits of forgiving yourself and others:

Maintenance Of Valuable Relationships

Forgiveness is the key that holds onto all relationships, whether interpersonal or professional. There would never have been any reason to forgive others if we could live in this world in isolation. However, it is not possible. According to Aristotle, only a beast or deity can be comfortable in isolation. So, we have to forgive our friends and families so that we don't lose them.

No matter how you love people, or they love you, they will hurt you at some point. Sometimes the hurt is minor while in some cases it can lead to an emotional wound that cuts deeply. Regardless of the nature of the hurt, you have to forgive to be able to sustain your relationships.

Sometimes when people hurt us, we would have forgotten all the good things they did in the past. If they have been good to us in the past, then they can still be helpful to us in the future if we give them another chance. Don't allow your emotions to determine your actions. You cannot deny the fact that their negative actions hurt you, but you have to forgive them to keep enjoying the camaraderie you had with them.

Expression Of Empathy

Empathy refers to the ability to put yourself in another's position. When you have empathy, you realize that you could have been in the same position as another person who is in an unpleasant situation. Forgiveness is one of the crucial ways to empathy. As human beings, we cannot be perfect. The best of us still do unimaginable things sometimes. When people hurt us, we should be honest enough to realize that we could have done the same thing.

Even if you have never hurt others the same way they hurt you, the truth is that you have done something that caused pain to someone else at some point or another. This honest admission of frailty is the foundation of empathy and it is what inspires forgiveness. It is hypocritical to refuse to forgive others when we have also wronged others before.

In a world full of imperfections, we need to keep our loved ones by forgiving them, regardless of what they have done. It is difficult to do this when you keep remembering the offence. Stop asking why they felt you deserved to be treated that way. It is an irrelevant question that will only deepen your reasons for not wanting to forgive.

Stability In Relationships

It is not a good thing when you can't keep relationships going. Why is everyone leaving you? Where are the people that used to be your friends five years ago? Why are you not on speaking terms with them any longer? If the reason is that they hurt you, then you need to work on yourself. You cannot keep changing friends because they did things you don't like to you.

If you are like that, you will never have loyal friends. It might also affect your marriage. There are cases where people divorce because one party is physically and emotionally abusing the other consistently. However, many marriages lead to divorce because the couple refused to forgive one another until it all piled up to the point where they felt breaking up was the best solution.

There is no relationship in the world where the people involved don't have reasons to be unhappy. If you speak to some of the people you feel are best friends or lovely couples living in solitude for years, you will realize that they have had issues in the past. The only reason two people stay by themselves for a long time is that they refuse to give up on themselves.

Physical And Mental Heart

When you carry hurt in your heart, it can affect your physical and mental health. You can develop depression when you keep thinking about the terrible incident. Meanwhile, depression is a severe mental health issue, affecting over 264 million people around the world, according to the World Health Organization (WHO).

When you are not happy, it might affect your eating habits and make you incapable of engaging in exercise. So, forgiving is always to your benefit. It frees you from the burden that is making your life miserable and empowers you to live the happy, healthy, and meaningful life you deserve. According to a study by the John Hopkins hospital, forgiveness has major health benefits.

Inner Peace

Whatever takes away your peace has robbed you of one of the most important things in your life. Unforgiveness makes you carry a burden that holds you bound to the person that hurt you and makes you incapable of enjoying your life. It holds you captive, like a prisoner. Your mood changes immediately when you remember the person. No matter how happy you are, your mood will change immediately when you see the person, or you remember what the person did to you.

In some cases, you might have nightmares about the incident because our dreams are often products of our thoughts. You have become a slave to the hurt. It now controls your mood and has the power to ruin your day. For your own sake, forgive the person so that you can move on with your life.

No one should hold the power to your peace and happiness, and you should never allow anyone to wield such power over you. The best way to avoid such a situation is to forgive and let go of the past. Acknowledge the pain but don't let it define you. Don't let it become the reference point to when you lost yourself and your smile. A 2020 study showed that forgiveness eliminates resentment and anger.

Personal Happiness

If you keep thinking about the betrayal or denial by someone you trusted, you will not be able to think straight. As the incident continues to play on your mind, you will find it difficult to go about your daily activities as expected. Whenever you remember the incident, it will be as though you are watching the scene of a horror movie.

You don't deserve to live your life in sadness and regret. However, the ball is in your court. You can either choose to make a particularly devastating event define your life and ruin your future, or you can choose to let go of the past and plan for a better future that enables you to live your life to the fullest. A 2010 study confirmed that forgiveness ultimately contributes to well-being.

Chapter Three: Forgiving Yourself

"Forgiveness is a gift you give yourself."
Suzanne Somers

If you don't learn to forgive yourself, it can eventually make you take your own life. So, it is a reality you need to fight against, and forgiving yourself plays a crucial role in this. The tips below will help you in this regard:

You Are Fallible

Perfection is an illusion that is not attainable. It is crucial that you put in your best to avoid mistakes and you should be meticulous enough to cut out errors. Yet, the reality is that you will make mistakes at some point or another. It is just human nature. The reality is that errors are usually costly and that is why it hurts when we commit them.

Your mistake might cost you dearly and in some cases it might also affect the people that trust you. During the Euros 2020, played among European national football teams, Bukayo Saka, Jando Sancho, and Marcus Rashford missed the penalties that cost England the final test against Italy. There is no doubt that this mistake would hurt them because it cost their team valuable points and also affected the hopes of the nation of winning the competition.

Yet, they cannot afford to allow the mistake to define them. Kylian Mpabbe of France also missed a penalty that cost his team. This is a player who is considered one of the finest talents of his generation. That is just life. Making mistakes that can be costly is all part of life and you should not feel like you have done something unpardonable. Even if others don't forgive you, you have to forgive yourself. During the same competition, Frello Jorginho, a player considered to be one of the finest penalty takers in the world, also missed a penalty. Fortunately for him, it didn't cost his team.

There Are Others Like You

In the case of the English trio of Sancho, Saka, and Rashford, they must have noticed that other stellar names, like Mbappe and Jorginho also missed their penalties. Cristiano Ronaldo and Lionel Messi have also missed penalties before, even though they are regarded as two of the finest players to have ever played football. That's life! If you are observant enough, you will realize that some of the people you adore have also made the same mistakes you made before.

So, don't feel like the end has come because you did something you ought not to have done. Even when you hurt the people that love and trust you, you just have to move on. If you move on, life will give you another opportunity to make up for your past mistakes. If you did something wrong, you should apologize when necessary, but you should never allow anyone to make you feel that you have committed an unpardonable offence.

No offence is unpardonable. Others might not forgive you and in some cases, the law of the land might not be merciful to you. Still, you should forgive yourself. Crying and feeling sad about what you did in the past will not change the situation. It will only affect your mental and physical health. Apologize when necessary, but never fail to move on

Learn The Lessons

It is foolish not to take advantage of our experiences, to make better decisions in the future. Your mistakes can be a blessing in disguise if you choose to learn from them. Experience can be a nasty teacher because it teaches you bitter lessons but the good thing about its crude method is that you will never forget the lessons.

It leaves a sour taste in the mouth that reminds you about the consequences of doing such things. So, if you find yourself in a situation where you did something you know you should not have done, take advantage of it. Never waste an experience. Don't be too quick to move one. You have to move on but you need to reflect on what you did first before you do so.

Think about the reasons you made the mistake. Was it due to peer pressure, lack of adequate information, hastiness, or overconfidence? It is when you can provide the right answer to this question that you will be able to make better decisions in the future. If not, you will keep making the same mistakes, which doesn't speak well of your level of intelligence or emotional maturity.

Take Responsibility

You are a product of the decisions you make. So, when you make bad decisions, it is true that it would have some negative impact on you. There will be situations where the things you did in the past will make some people deny you certain opportunities, but you should not let that affect you. You should be willing to take responsibility for your actions.

Acknowledge that you did the wrong thing but don't let it define your future. Even your strongest critic will be persuaded eventually when you are consistent in your new lifestyle. Normally, people would doubt you initially. You cannot blame them. They just want to be careful because nobody wants to get hurt, especially when you have hurt them in the past.

Don't expect your spouse to give you another chance immediately, just because you claim that you are a new person. You should expect that he or she will keep watching you. If you continue to act well, you may get another chance again. Don't promise or do things you know are not sustainable, just to impress others. Be yourself and continue to grow. The future is bright if only you don't give up.

You Can Still Turn Things Around

One of the greatest hindrances to forgiving yourself and moving on is when you feel that all hope is lost. Don't listen to that lying voice in your head telling you that you can never amount to anything again because of your past mistakes. As long as you are still alive, there is still hope for you. Never get to that point where you feel that things have gotten too messy.

There is still an opportunity to redeem yourself as long as you are still alive. Find inspiration from the stories of others. Some people have been in your situation before and turned it around. Let the story of such people give you the motivation you need to make the best out of your life. No matter what, find reasons to keep fighting for forgiveness.

Even if no one is backing you, have confidence in yourself because it is your life at the end of the day. You should be grateful to the people that support you and encourage you to make the best of your life. Yet, what matters most is your commitment to living a happy life.

Chapter Four: Forgiving Others

"It's not an easy journey to get to a place where you forgive people but it is such a powerful place because it frees you."

Tyler Perry

Forgiving others indeed becomes easier when you learn to forgive yourself. Yet, you must know how to go about it. In this chapter, we will discuss certain things you need to understand that will enhance your ability to forgive others.

Forgiveness Is Not A Sign Of Weakness

In the words of T.D. Jakes, "We think that forgiveness is weakness, but it's not; it takes a very strong-minded person to forgive." One of the old mindsets that fuels unforgiveness is that the act of forgiving is a sign of a weak character. This is far from the truth. The reality is that it is easier to take revenge than to forgive. When people hurt you, you are naturally inclined to want to take your pound of flesh. You just want to satisfy your emotions.

Choosing to forgive is often like a fight. It feels like you are restraining the urge to do something natural. Forgiveness is a process that involves self-control and self-discipline, which many people lack. Vengeance is instant gratification, which is natural to us but forgiveness is delayed gratification, emotional maturity, which pays off in the long run. In most cases, you don't see the benefit of choosing to forgive immediately and that is why many people don't resort to it.

Revenge can feel sweet immediately but it is always distasteful in the long run, while forgiveness can be bitter initially because of how you feel but you will be proud that you did it, eventually. Weak people prefer the instant gratification that comes with vengeance, while strong people choose the delayed but long-lasting gratification that comes with forgiving others.

The People You Love Hurt You More

What hurts the most is when the people you love and trust break your heart. It is not shocking when strangers hurt you because you don't know them, and it is expected that they might misjudge you and do or say mean things to you. It is easier to ignore the harsh words of a social media personality that is not close to you. You might see it as just one of those things people do to get fame and "likes" on social media.

However, it is more difficult to accept when your friends say mean things about you. In the case study of Lovely Peaches and Charli D'Amelio. The words of Lovely

Peaches might not mean so much to Charli because she doesn't know her personally. However, things would be different if Dixie, her sister, said the same things. She would be disappointed because of the close relationship they have as siblings.

We don't expect our loved ones to hurt us and that is why we feel more pain when they do. One of the ways you can reduce the pain that comes with the disappointment of the betrayal or wrong actions of a loved one is to expect that it can happen. This mindset will serve as a shock-absorber and buffer that will help you to recover and find it easier to forgive them when they hurt you.

Find Out Why

One of the reasons people struggle to forgive their loved ones is that they are not interested in the reason they hurt them. They assume that they changed and decided to hurt them for no reason apart from the fact that they suddenly became mean. This is not true. Things don't just happen. In some cases, your loved ones hurt you unintentionally. Sometimes, they do the things that hurt you without knowing that you would feel that way.

So, by asking them why they acted that way, you might be able to understand what went wrong. If your romantic partner decided to call it quits, don't just throw in the towel. Sometimes, the person is not sure about the decision. He or she might be under parental and peer pressure, which you are not aware of. Sometimes, they are afraid that they might not be able to take care of you in the future.

When you find out why they made the decision, you might be able to forgive them. In some cases, people do the wrong things to you to get back at you for treating them badly in the past. When you try to understand the reason for their actions, it might help you to avoid acting in such ways that might make you the target of hurtful words or actions. It will also help you to resolve issues and forgive more easily.

Do It For Yourself

It is not everyone that hurts you who will be willing to offer you an explanation for their actions. In some cases, finding out why they hurt might even make you angrier. Still, you have no other choice but to forgive them. Note that the primary reason for forgiving others is not for them but for you. You need to forgive others so that you don't have reasons to carry burdens of pain and hurt in your heart.

Some people erroneously claim that you should only forgive the people that deserve it. This is far from the truth because no one deserves to be forgiven. Whoever decided to hurt another person for one reason or the other does not deserve to be forgiven. They deserve punishment and pain. Yet, you must not be vengeful and full of anger because it is not good for your mental and physical health.

So, that thinking that forgiveness is only meant for the people that deserve it is faulty. Do you remember the opening quote in chapter one of this book by Jonathan Huie? The essence of forgiveness is that you deserve peace. Therefore, even if you cannot find any other reason you should stop hating someone, do it for yourself.

Be Willing To Try Again

Many people claim that we can only forgive but cannot forget. Well, it is true to an extent because it is not as though you suffered memory loss that will wipe away the remembrance of the action. So, it is normal if you remember what the person did but you must not continue to see it in the same way. Don't keep remembering an unpleasant memory in the same light. Instead, treat it as something that happened in the past that is no longer relevant to the present.

This will make you give people another chance to mend their ways. You have not truly forgiven a person until you are willing to give them another chance, if possible. What I mean by if possible is that some chances are gone because of the current reality. For example, if your spouse hurts you and it leads to a divorce, you will not be able to give him or her another chance if you are already remarried by the time the person comes to his or her senses.

However, there are situations where you can allow the person to try again, especially if the person is a friend. We all want to have another chance to show that we have turned over a new leaf and we ought to allow others to have the same opportunity. After forgiveness, you have to be willing to try again. It is okay if you want to take things slowly, but you must not shut the door.

Chapter Five: Law Of Advance Forgiveness

"Anger begets more anger, and forgiveness and love lead to more forgiveness and love."
Mahavira

In this chapter, we will talk about the law of advance forgiveness. It is a crucial rule that serves as a buffer that makes it easier for you to forgive. It involves forgiving people even before they offend you. This is the height of forgiveness and only a few people have reached this level in the school of forgiveness. The following tips will help you to attain this elusive but lofty level:

Expect To Be Offended

If you want to practice the law of advance forgiveness, you must also expect to be offended. This is not negative thinking. Expecting that people will offend you is being realistic and it is an effective way to prevent the strong feeling of disappointment that makes people feel that they cannot forgive certain people because of what they did to them. Whether you expect it or not, people will offend you. So, you should prepare your mind for it so that you can have enough in your emotional tank to be able to forgive them.

There is a metaphorical emotional tank we all have from which we draw out positive emotions. This tank contains love, forgiveness, and happiness. When you have enough in this tank, you will still be able to love and forgive others, which enables you to live a happy life even when they have done something very painful to you. On the other hand, when this tank is empty or almost empty, all you will have to give is hatred and vengeance. One of the ways you can ensure that you always have this in the reserve is to expect that your loved ones will offend you.

Think The Unthinkable

We are all keen to avoid negative thoughts and it is a good approach to life. It is not healthy to fill your mind with thoughts of anger and disappointment if you want to live the happy and meaningful life you desire. Yet, it is not every time you think about something negative that it necessarily makes it negative thinking. There are times that you have to contemplate the possibility of something unpleasant happening. This does not mean that you are expecting it to happen. Most importantly, you shouldn't delve into the realm of self-prophesy of those things.

Still, you must contemplate the other side of something positive so that you can prepare your mind for every eventuality. For example, even when you are in a harmonious relationship where your partner treats you well, you should let your mind wander sometimes to evaluate your response if things turn sour. Ask yourself what you will do if your spouse cheats on you and ignores you. Will you forgive him or her? Will you try to find out the cause of the problem and find a means to restore your relationship? If you can plan to forgive people ahead by thinking about the possibility of them acting funny, you will not struggle to forgive them if they eventually hurt you.

Realize The Fallibility Of Your Loved Ones

Some people can treat you so well and act in such a loyal way toward you, that you quickly forget that they are human beings. People cannot be perfect and you have to realize that. Don't wait until they display their imperfections before you realize that they have weaknesses too. You should not try to seek the weaknesses or downfall of your loved ones but it is important to know their specific deficiencies. Once you know them, it becomes easier to know what to expect from them.

This will make you plan to love them despite their weaknesses. It is because people are caught by surprise when their loved ones act in certain ways that make them struggle to forgive them. You should know the areas where your friends and families are weakest and love them all the same. This is the foundation of every harmonious relationship.

Plan To Forgive Ahead

No relationship is perfect. Best of friends argue and say mean things to one another sometimes. Forgiveness is the key that ensures that we maintain our friendships with people. Without forgiveness, we can never form strong bonds with others. People will always be people and you should never forget that. We are fallible and our frailties can show up in very abysmal ways. What we all need are people that can love us, especially on those days we do stupid things.

I am sure that you want to have such friends. If that is the case, why can't you be that kind of person to your loved ones? We all want people to love us for who we are and allow us to grow but many of us are too quick to judge others. We don't give them the benefit of the doubt or cut them some slack, but we want the same from them. That's hypocritical. You should be the kind of friend that you want others to be to you. Always plan to forgive ahead of the, before it happens, once you know the weaknesses of your loved ones.

Refuse To Give Up On Your Relationships

Harmonious relationships are not magical. They are built on the investments of two or more people that refused to give up on one another. Due to the rate of divorce in the modern world, many people are already giving up on marriage. Many young people believe that it is a fraudulent institution where people never show who they are until they have exchanged vows. The truth is that marriage has not changed. What has changed is the way people handle it.

We seem to have too many people that are impatient in the modern world. They break up a relationship at the slightest sight of trouble and turbulence. Relationships are like ships. There will be periods that they will have to weather the storm. What will determine whether it will sink or keep sailing is the collective effort of the parties involved. If the people involved in a relationship refuse to give up on one another, nothing can break it. You can plan to refuse to give up on your relationships, no matter what happens.

Always Seek Reconciliation

Many people have this notion that whoever has hurt them must beg them first before they forgive that person. This is not the best approach. It is not a big deal if you approach the person that has offended you, first. It takes a high level of emotional maturity that many people don't possess today. Many people in the world are like cranky children that keep sulking whenever somebody hurts them.

If you value the relationship you have with a person, it is not a crime if you are the first to seek reconciliation, even when the other person is at fault. You don't have to be at fault to seek reconciliation. Once you learn this approach, you will realize that the people around you will respect you more because they will realize that you have an advanced level of maturity.

Chapter Six: Avoiding Offences

"When a deep injury is done to us, we never recover until we forgive."
Alan Paton

It is a fantastic attribute to possess when you are willing to take responsibility for your actions and apologize, but it is better to avoid hurting people in the first place. We have been dealing with forgiving ourselves and others but in this chapter, we will explore how to avoid offending others. This is crucial because people hurt us sometimes. After all, we hurt them in the first place too at times. As seen from the quote above, hurting others can be a form of a deep injury. Indeed, they have to forgive to recover but it is better to avoid hurting them. The tips below will help you in this regard:

Clear Expectations

You cannot please a person when you don't know what the person wants. Only a lunatic or maniac gets angry for no reason. People don't just treat you badly; there is always a reason for their actions, and you need to find out so that you don't get on their wrong side. In your relationships, take time to study the other party. Try to understand the likes and dislikes of the other person so that you can know how best to approach them.

You must understand the level of emotional development of your friends and family members. Some people can respond well, even when they are going through tough times, while some people get cranky and angry when things are not going their way. If you know that your friend often says mean things when he is experiencing a bad moment, avoid talking to him as much as possible during that period. Even if you want to correct that attitude, wait until he is in a happy mood. He is likely to be defensive when he is not happy. So, wait for the right time so that the conversation can have the desired impact.

Clear Communication

By being observant, you can know what to expect from a person. Yet, being observant is not good enough because you might be assuming the reason an individual is acting in a particular way. Therefore, you must maintain an open line of communication with your loved ones. If they acted in a way that you couldn't understand, talk to them about it. Of course, the timing of every conversation is important. You should avoid talking to them during the periods they are busy or are not in a good mood, to have productive interactions with them.

Assumptions are dangerous in relationships. It is always better that you ask questions so that the person can tell you what he or she wants. This is one of the reasons some people find it difficult to get along with one another. People are not the same and you need to understand that. The fact that you did something to a particular friend and he or she didn't react doesn't mean that others will act that way too When you notice that a person reacted to something you did in a way you couldn't understand, find out why the person acted that way so that you can avoid such a situation in the future.

Listen More

It is excellent to have great communication skills, but it is more important to develop quality listening skills. Many people talk more than they listen, which is not good. You should rather listen more than speak. Note that listening is not the same as hearing.

Hearing doesn't require concerted effort. As long as your auditory system is functional, you will hear when people speak. However, you have to be deliberate about *listening* to others.

Listening is difficult for many people because they like to hear the sound of their own voices. They lack the patience that is necessary to consider the opinion of others and act accordingly. If you don't have excellent listening skills, you will struggle in your relationships. When people observe that you listen to them, they will see you as a respectful person that values their opinion, which makes it easier for them to open up to you. They will be more willing to tell you when they feel there are certain things you need to avoid so that you will not hurt them, which is vital to the sustenance of your interpersonal relationships.

Let What Matters To Others Matter To You

You cannot claim that you love a person when you don't value the things that matter to them. If you love me, you have to love my children, wife, friends, and family. This does not mean that you have to agree with them on everything. Still, you cannot claim that you respect me and then disrespect my spouse. The fact that I mean something to you should be more than enough reason that you should value whatever concerns me. This is an integral part that many people fail to understand in their interpersonal relationships.

One of the easiest ways to avoid hurting others is to value the things that matter to them. By observing and asking questions, you will be able to know the things that your friends and family hold in high esteem. Even if you don't have the same level of respect for those things, you should not talk down to them or speak about them in a derogatory manner. It is better that you say nothing about those things in their presence, instead of rocking the boat by saying mean things about them.

Develop The Heart Of a Servant

You should not be too afraid that you might hurt your loved ones, but it should matter to you that they see you as a blessing in their lives. One of the best ways you can do this is by developing a servant's heart. This implies that you are that friend that your loved ones can always count on to help them when they are in need. You mustn't do this because you expect them to do something for you in return. This transactional mindset is one of the things that ruin relationships.

Some people have a terrible habit of doing things for their friends and family so that they can get something in return. This is only acceptable in the business world. It is when you work in a company that you have to expect that you get paid. You should not carry over this thinking to your interpersonal relationships. You can easily become that person that everyone wants to have around them when you make it a habit to add value to their lives. It will inspire your friends and family to also reciprocate your good deeds, but you should never expect it or demand it from them.

Chapter Seven: Reducing Chances Of Getting Hurt

"Forgive your enemy but never forget their name."

John F. Kennedy

It is commendable to have mastery over the art of not offending others. Yet, it is also vital that you know how to help the people around you in such a way that they will not hurt you. Your loved ones will inevitably hurt you, but you can reduce the chance of its occurrence by leveraging the following tips:

Make Reasonable Demands

You should be sacrificial in your relationships but that doesn't mean that you should be afraid to make demands. In other words, your friends and family should know the things that matter to you and you should not have issues telling them about those things. Of course, the way you go about it matters. You should avoid making demands in the heat of the moment. For example, the worst time to explain why you don't share your shoes is not when your friend has used them. Talking about it at that moment might make the person feel embarrassed.

It might make the person stop using your shoes but it can build up hard feelings that can escalate in the future. The way you handle an issue is very important. Wait till the moment the person will not be defensive and calmly explain why you don't share your shoes with other people. This will make the person understand how you feel without being tempted to get defensive, which can lead to arguments. You should not lose your friends because of something as ephemeral as shoes. Make reasonable demands so that your loved ones will know what you don't like but ensure that you go about it the right way.

Be Willing To Compromise

As much as you should have clear expectations in your relationships so that your loved ones will know your likes and dislikes, you don't always have to insist on your rights. This is one of the reasons romantic relationships and marriages break down. If you are living with your spouse, you cannot always expect to have things go your way. Of course, you should let the other person know how you feel about certain things so that the person can make adjustments. Still, you should be willing to shift ground, especially in areas that don't mean the world to you.

This will also encourage the other person to make compromises too so that you can continue to live together in harmony. You can be uncompromising in your business and that is fine. You should have standards for your business administration that you are convinced will increase the customer retention and loyalty of your organization. You should be committed to them and refuse to compromise on them. However, you cannot transfer that attitude to your interpersonal relationships. You should be willing to allow your loved ones to have their way on certain things sometimes, to avoid getting angry unnecessarily and consistently.

Keep Communicating

Don't expect that your friends and family will start doing something once you tell them to. Even when they agree with you that they would never act in a particular way again, they might still end up acting that way due to forgetfulness or other factors. When you notice this, you don't have to nag them. Still, you should mention it once in a while again so that they can remember the promise they made to you. The way you go about this is also important to avoid hounding your friends and family.

Don't remind them in an angry tone, stirring up negative emotions. If you notice that you are angry, don't say anything. You can take five deep breaths or use other anger management techniques. This is crucial because it is likely that you may say things when you are angry that you wish you had never said, later. This doesn't mean that you should not be firm. You can be firm and make demands without showing signs of anger and frustration. Speaking angrily will not help you or the recipient of your actions. If you notice that you often get angry easily, work on it before it ruins your relationships.

Train Before Delegating

Delegation enables you to do more within the time you have. You have to leverage it to reduce your stress level and improve your efficiency. Nonetheless, delegating tasks is one of the potential ways you can find yourself at loggerheads with others. It's important to trust the person that you are delegating the task to, before doing so. Ensure that the person is trained and capable of carrying out the task before you assign it to him or her. You should have the same approach regardless of whether you are paying the person or not.

When you outsource a task, you might be able to sue the person or get compensated for whatever damages are incurred while the person is carrying out the task. However, you might not be able to do so when you ask your friend or family to help out in carrying out a task on your behalf. So, to avoid getting angry and engaging in heated arguments, ensure that the person is trained to carry out the responsibility. You should be willing to train your loved ones so that they can be effective when helping you.

Test Before Trusting

You should trust people, but you shouldn't always take their word for it, especially when you are delegating sensitive tasks to them. Some people overestimate their ability to carry out certain responsibilities. Their overconfidence can make you trust them, but you will regret it eventually if you do so.

Before you commit a sensitive task to people, test them with something similar. Don't let the pressure of carrying out something urgently make you trust someone that would ruin the job. You will have to forgive the person then. So, it is better that you reduce the chances of getting hurt by only giving people vital responsibilities when they have been tested.

Chapter Eight: Just Be Happy!

"There is no revenge so complete like forgiveness"

Josh Billings

Happiness is the greatest pursuit of man and it is something that must not be missing from your life. The good news is that you can choose to be happy. Practicing forgiveness is one of the best ways you can choose to be happy. The tips in this chapter will help you in this regard.

Forgive! Forgive!! Forgive!!! And Forgive Again

Some people hurt you so that you can carry the burden for the rest of your life. They want you to know that they hate you and want your attention. A TikToker called Lovely Peaches has a culture of harassing people such as Charli D'Amelio online. She kept popping up in the comment section of Charli's videos to say mean things to her but Charli would never say a word to her in return.

This is the best way to treat a hater. It hurts them more when you don't respond to them. Some people want to be your weak point, especially when you are successful. Their success comes from being described as your Achilles Heel or pain in the neck. Don't allow them to get that opportunity. Jose Mourinho is a wonderful football manager, but he has a culture of getting under the skin of managers by making annoying comments about their team.

For years, he used this mind game tactic to ruffle the feathers of opponents before a game even began. There are always people like that in the world. They would deliberately say things that would annoy you so that they can distract you and gain an advantage. It is best for you if you ignore such people. You cannot ignore them if you don't forgive them. When you try to hit back at them, you might make a mistake that you would regret. When that happens, they have achieved what they wanted and you would become a laughing stock.

Vengeance Is Not An Option

Don't let anyone deceive you; revenge is not sweet! It is bitter and it can cause more damage to you than you realize. It can turn you into a monster. You will not believe what you can transform into when you refuse to forgive. The thought of vengeance will make you incapable of living a happy life. It will fill your heart with anger and hate until you take your pound of flesh.

The issue with vengeance is that it usually never has an end. When someone hurts you, and you hurt them back, chances are very high that the person will plan a counterattack, which might be more devastating than what you did to them. Besides, the desire for vengeance can lead you into a life of crime that might make you spend the most productive part of your life in jail.

Many people are so clouded with the thoughts of revenge that they stop thinking logically. That is until they have hurt the person that they later realize they should have let go. When you cannot overlook offences, you are a potential liability to your team. In a football game, bad-tempered players often get a lot of red cards that put their team at a disadvantage. Their problem is that they never overlook offences. They would be so consumed with the desire for revenge, that they would not think about how their actions can hurt their team's opportunity to win.

Stay Away From Vengeful People

We are all products of influence. Your relationship with others is like a chemical reaction; it will always produce a new product. The easiest way to have the boldness to do certain things that you thought you could never do is to stay around people that do such things. This same rule applies to bad habits, such as smoking and good habits, such as diligence in one's career.

It is in the same way you can learn to give by staying around positive people, that you can also pick up the bad habit of being vengeful by staying around angry people. Such people will fan the flames of your desire for revenge after others have hurt you. We all want to be around the people that would commend us. Sadly, when you are around vengeful people, they would commend you for hurting others and taking revenge.

In the words of Lecrae Moore, "They said I am good at bad things; at least they are proud of me." Don't hang around the people that praise you for doing the wrong things and call you a fool when you do the right things. Once their validation means a lot to you, you will always do the wrong things so that they can commend you. Note people that pour praise on you when you take revenge and stay away from them.

Make Friends That Encourage You To Forgive

Staying away from vengeful people is not enough because you must fill every vacuum and void in your life. You need to have friends. Still, you have to be careful about the way you go about it. Ensure that your friends are people that can encourage you to forgive others when they hurt you.

You need such people, especially on those days you feel too weak to forgive because you were shocked that someone you trusted and loved so much could hurt you so deeply. Good friends are needed most on dark days. You need such people on those days that you are fighting the desire for revenge. Their emotional support will see you through on such days.

Keep Unrepentant People At Arm's Length

You should always believe the best about others and you should always allow them to mend their ways. However, you have to be careful so that people don't keep making it tough for you to forgive them. It is not very clever when you don't learn from the past. If people claim that they have turned over a new leaf, give them a chance but don't give them the same level of trust and access they had before.

Trust should be earned. It shouldn't be something you give every Tom, Dick, and Harry. It is okay when people apologize to you after they hurt you but it is not an apology that you should prioritize. What should matter more to you is repentance. You should watch out for a change of behaviour and character before you give people the same level of trust and access you once gave them.

You only live once and you deserve to be happy. Don't let anyone take that away from you. Never stop forgiving your loved ones. Remember that they are the ones that are likely to hurt you the most because of the access and trust you give them. Yet, you don't have to stay close to a person if the person is not willing to turn over a new leaf. Only stay around the people that value you.

Conclusion

I am convinced that you are glad that you read this book at this point. You would have realized that forgiveness is not as difficult as many people think it is. Once you focus on the fact that the greatest beneficiary of forgiveness is you, it becomes easier to practice this salient art.

We began this journey by intimating that the concept of forgiveness is important to your life and the reason for that. It is the key that unlocks your happiness, which you must never lose. We also discussed how you need to forgive yourself so that you can find it easier to forgive others.

The chapter on the law of advance forgiveness is very vital because it gives you enough fuel in your emotional tank to let go of future offences. We also discussed how you can avoid offending others and how you can also ensure that others don't make you sad. They are two sides of the forgiveness coin that you have to master. Reading this book is not enough. Ensure that you practice what you have learned and watch yourself transform from that ugly caterpillar to a beautiful butterfly.

References

WHO. (2021, June 17). *Depression.* https://www.who.int/health-topics/depression

Forgiveness: Your Health Depends on It. (n.d.). Johns Hopkins Medicine. Retrieved September 22, 2021, from https://www.hopkinsmedicine.org/health/wellness-and-prevention/forgiveness-your-health-depends-on-it

Long, K.N.G., Worthington, E.L., VanderWeele, T.J. et al. Forgiveness of others and subsequent health and well-being in mid-life: a longitudinal study on female nurses. BMC Psychol 8, 104 (2020). https://doi.org/10.1186/s40359-020-00470-w

Sutton, J., Ph.D. (2020, October 21). *Psychology of Forgiveness: 10+ Fascinating Research Findings.* PositivePsychology.Com. https://positivepsychology.com/psychology-of-forgiveness/

The New Science of Forgiveness. (2004). Greater Good. https://greatergood.berkeley.edu/article/item/the_new_science_of_forgiveness

Thank you for reading this book!

If you found this book helpful, I would be grateful if you would **post an honest review on Amazon** so this book can reach other supportive readers like you!

All you need to do is digitally flip to the back and leave your review. Or visit amazon.com/author/senseipauldavid click the correct book cover and click on the blue link next to the yellow stars that says, "customer reviews."

As always...
It's a great day to be alive!

Get/Share Our FREE All-Ages Mental Health Book Now!

FREE Self-Development Book for Every Family

senseiselfdevelopment.senseipublishing.com

Click Below or Search Amazon for Another Book In This Series Or Visit:

www.amazon.com/author/senseipauldavid

www.senseipublishing.com

@senseipublishing
#senseipublishing

Check out our **recommendations** for other books for adults & kids plus other great resources by visiting
www.senseipublishing.com/resources/

Join Our Publishing Journey!

If you would like to receive FREE BOOKS, special offers, please visit www.senseipublishing.com and join our newsletter by entering your email address in the pop-up box

Follow Our Engaging Blog NOW! senseipauldavid.ca

Get Our FREE Books Today!

Click & Share the Link Below

FREE Self-Development Book
senseiselfdevelopment.senseipublishing.com

FREE BONUS!!!
Experience Over 25 FREE Engaging Guided Meditations!

Prized Skills & Practices for Adults & Kids. Help Restore Deep-Sleep, Lower Stress, Improve Posture, Navigate Uncertainty & More.

Download the Free Insight Timer App and click the link below:
http://insig.ht/sensei_paul

About Sensei Publishing

Sensei Publishing commits itself to help people of all ages transform into better versions of themselves by providing high-quality and research-based self-development books with an emphasis on mental health and guided meditations. Sensei Publishing offers well-written e-books, audiobooks, paperbacks and online courses that simplify complicated but practical topics in line with its mission to inspire people towards positive transformation.

It's a great day to be alive!

About the Author

I create simple & transformative eBooks & Guided Meditations for Adults & Children proven to help navigate uncertainty, solve niche problems & bring families closer together.

I'm a former finance project manager, private pilot, jiu-jitsu instructor, musician & former University of Toronto Fitness Trainer. I prefer a science-based approach to focus on these & other areas in my life to stay humble & hungry to evolve. I hope you enjoy my work and I'd love to hear your feedback.

- It's a great day to be alive!
Sensei Paul David

Scan & Follow/Like/Subscribe:
Facebook, Instagram, YouTube:
@senseipublishing

Scan using your phone/iPad camera for Social Media Visit us at www.senseipublishing.com and sign up to our newsletter to learn more about our exciting books and to experience our FREE Guided Meditations for Kids & Adults.

www.ingramcontent.com/pod-product-compliance
Lightning Source LLC
Chambersburg PA
CBHW062140100526
44589CB00014B/1632